Shine & Sparkle by Arlene Williams

Published by URDeziin, LLC

400 W Peachtree Street, St 4. Atlanta, GA 30308

www.urdeziinevolution.com

Cover by URDeziin, LLC.

Credits: Jimmie Williams, Yahvette Richardson

INTRODUCTION

- Change your life now with these affirmations
- These affirmations can be read every day to help build a positive spiritual life.
- Give your life a positive twist and start living life to the fullest.
- Boost your self-esteem and build self-confidence.
- Get positive affirmations to uplift you daily.
- Get positive affirmations to help you feel confident.

AFFIRMATIONS ABOUT FAITH

- And all things, whatsoever ye shall ask in prayer, believing, ye shall receive. And when he was come into the Temple, the chief priests and the elders of the people came unto him as he was teaching, and said, By what authority do you these things? and who gave you this authority? MATTITHYAHU (MATTHEW) 21:22-23 את CEPHER

- So then faith comes by hearing, and hearing by the Word of Elohiym. ROMAIYM (ROMANS) 10:17 את CEPHER

- But without faith it is impossible to please him: for he that comes to Elohiym must believe that he is, and that he is a rewarder of them that diligently seek him. IVRIYM (HEBREWS) 11:6 את CEPHER

- And Yahusha answering said unto them, Have faith in Elohiym. For amein I say unto you, That whosoever shall say unto this mountain, Be removed, and be cast into the sea; and shall not doubt in his heart, but shall believe that those things which he says shall come to pass; he shall have whatsoever he says. Therefore I say unto you, What things soever ye desire, when ye pray, believe that ye receive them, and ye shall have them. MARQUS (MARK) 11:22-24 את CEPHER

- You believe that there is one Elohiym; you do well: the devils also believe, and tremble. YA`AQOV (JAMES) 2:19 את CEPHER

- NOW faith is the substance of things hoped for, the evidence of things not seen. IVRIYM (HEBREWS) 11:1 את CEPHER

- For with Elohiym nothing shall be impossible. LUQAS (LUKE) 1:37 את CEPHER For by grace are ye saved through faith; and that not of yourselves: it is the gift of Elohiym: Not of works, lest any man should boast. EPH'SIYM (EPHESIANS) 2:8-9 את

CEPHER

- Trust in El-Yahuah with all your heart; and lean not unto your own understanding. In all your ways acknowledge him, and he shall direct your paths. MISHLEI (PROVERBS) 3:5-6 את CEPHER

- NOW faith is the substance of things hoped for, the evidence of things not seen. IVRIYM (HEBREWS) 11:1 את CEPHER

- That your faith should not stand in the wisdom of men, but in the power of Elohiym. QORINTIYM RI'SHON (1 CORINTHIANS) 2:5 את CEPHER

- (For we walk by faith, not by sight:) QORINTIYM SHENIY (2 CORINTHIANS) 5:7 את CEPHER

- What does it profit, my brethren, though a man say he has faith, and have not works? can faith save him? If a brother or sister be naked, and destitute of daily food, YA`AQOV (JAMES) 2:14-15 את CEPHER

- If any of you lack wisdom, let him ask of Elohiym, that gives to all men liberally, and upbraids not; and it shall be given him. But let him ask in faith, nothing wavering. For he that wavers is like a wave of the sea driven with the wind and tossed. For let not that man think that he shall receive anything of Yahuah. A double minded man is unstable in all his ways. YA`AQOV (JAMES) 1:5-8 את CEPHER

Time to walk out your faith...

- When you wake up in the morning, tell yourself that you're a positive person.
- Remind yourself to be grateful for all you have, no matter how small or large.
- Tell yourself that all your fears are completely irrational and have no basis in reality.
- Tell yourself that all your worries can be set aside and will disappear because of your positive outlook on life.
- Remind yourself that you have nothing to worry about and that you're a kind, generous, and thoughtful person.
- Repeat this process every morning and watch your life turn around in a positive way.

AFFIRMATIONS ABOUT LOVE

- Love suffers long, and is kind; love envies not; love does not vaunt itself, is not puffed up, Does not behave itself unseemly, את seeks not her own, is not easily provoked, thinks no evil; Rejoices not in iniquity, but rejoices in the Truth; Bears all things, believes all things, hopes all things, endures all things. Love never fails: but whether there be prophecies, they shall fail; whether there be tongues, they shall cease; whether there be knowledge, it shall vanish away. QORINTIYM RI'SHON 13:4-8 את CEPHER

- Let all your things be done with love. QORINTIYM RI'SHON 16:14-14 את CEPHER

- He that loves not knows not Elohiym; for Elohiym is love. YOCHANON RI'SHON 4:8-8 את CEPHER

- And Yahusha answered him, The first of all the commandments is, Hear, O Yashar'el; Yahuah Elohaynu, Yahuah is one: And you shall love את Yahuah Elohayka with all your heart, and with all your soul, and with all your mind, and with all your strength: this is the first commandment. And the second is like, namely this, You shall love your neighbor as yourself. There is none other commandment greater than these. MARQUS 12:29-31 את CEPHER.

- Rabbi, which is the great commandment in the Torah? Yahusha said unto him, You shall love את Yahuah Elohayka with all your heart, and with all your soul, and with all your mind. This is the first and great commandment. And the second is like unto it, You shall love your neighbor as yourself. On these two commandments hang all the Torah and the prophets. MATTITHYAHU 22:36-40 את CEPHER

- A new commandment I give unto you, That ye love one another; as I have loved you, that ye also love one another. By this shall all men know that ye are my Talmidiym, if ye have love one to another. YOCHANON 13:34-35 את CEPHER

- And above all these things put on love, which is the bond of perfectness. QOLASIYM 3:14-14 את CEPHER
- Greater love has no man than this, that a man lay down his life for his friends. YOCHANON 15:13-13 את CEPHER
- For Elohiym so loved the world, that he gave his yachiyd, that whosoever believes in him should not perish, but have everlasting life. YOCHANON 3:16-16 את CEPHER
- We love him, because he first loved us. YOCHANON RI'SHON 4:19-19 את CEPHER
- Beloved, let us love one another: for love is of Elohiym; and everyone that loves is born of Elohiym, and knows את Elohiym. YOCHANON RI'SHON 4:7-7 את CEPHER
- And above all things have fervent love among yourselves: for love shall cover the multitude of sins. KEPHA RI'SHON 4:8-8 את CEPHER
- THOUGH I speak with the tongues of men and of angels, and have not love, I am become as sounding brass, or a tinkling cymbal. And though I have the gift of prophecy, and understand all mysteries, and all knowledge; and though I have all faith, so that I could remove mountains, and have not love, I am nothing. And though I bestow all my goods to feed the poor, and though I give my body to be burned, and have not love, it profits me nothing. Love suffers long, and is kind; love envies not; love does not vaunt itself, is not puffed up, Does not behave itself unseemly, את seeks not her own, is not easily provoked, thinks no evil; Rejoices not in iniquity, but rejoices in the Truth; QORINTIYM RI'SHON 13:1-6 את CEPHER
- Bears all things, believes all things, hopes all things, endures all things. Love never fails: but whether there be prophecies, they shall fail; whether there be tongues, they shall cease; whether there be knowledge, it shall vanish away. For we know in part, and we prophesy in part. But when that which is perfect is come, then that which is in part shall be done away. When I was a child, I spoke as a child, I understood

as a child, I thought as a child: but when I became a man, I put away childish things. For now we see through a glass, darkly; but then face to face: now I know in part; but then shall I know even as also I am known. QORINTIYM RI'SHON 13:7-12 את CEPHER

- And now abides faith, hope, love, these three; but the greatest of these is love. QORINTIYM RI'SHON 13:13-13 את CEPHER

TIME TO WALK OUT YOUR LOVE...

- Love yourself first and foremost Love others unconditionally Love your work, but do not be consumed by it Love your life, just as it is right now
- Write down 3-5 positive things that you love about yourself every day.
- Write down 3-5 positive things that you love about your significant other every day.
- Write down 3-5 positive things that you love about your family every day
- Write down 3-5 positive things that you love about your friends every day
- Write down 3-5 positive things that you love about your job every day.
- Write down 3-5 positive things that you love about your hobbies/interests every day.
- Write down 3-5 positive things that you love about your life every day.
- Review your list of positive things everyday and imagine each thing as if it was happening at that moment.
- Repeat the list every day for a month.
- Find new things daily to apply this to.

AFFIRMATIONS ABOUT HOPE

- Rejoicing in hope; patient in tribulation; continuing instant in prayer; ROMAIYM 12:12-12 את CEPHER
- Now the Elohiym of hope fill you with all joy and peace in believing, that ye may abound in hope, through the power of the Ruach Ha'Qodesh. ROMAIYM 15:13-13 את CEPHER
- For I know the thoughts that I think toward you, says Yahuah, thoughts of peace, and not of evil, to give you an expected end. YIRMEYAHU 29:11-11 את CEPHER
- By whom also we have access by faith into this grace wherein we stand, and rejoice in hope of the glory of Elohiym. And not only so, but we glory in tribulations also: knowing that tribulation works patience; And patience, experience; and experience, hope: And hope makes not ashamed; because the love of Elohiym is shed abroad in our hearts by the Ruach Ha'Qodesh which is given unto us. ROMAIYM 5:2-5 את CEPHER
- Be strong and of a good courage, fear not, nor be afraid of them: for Yahuah Elohayka, he it is that goes with you; he will not fail you, nor forsake you. DEVARIYM 31:6-6 את CEPHER
- But they that wait upon Yahuah shall renew their strength; they shall mount up with wings as eagles; they shall run, and not be weary; and they shall walk, and not faint. YESHA'YAHU 40:31-31 את CEPHER
- Rejoicing in hope; patient in tribulation; continuing instant in prayer; ROMAIYM 12:12-12 את CEPHER
- Now the Elohiym of hope fill you with all joy and peace in believing, that ye may abound in hope, through the power of the Ruach Ha'Qodesh. ROMAIYM 15:13-13 את CEPHER
- For I know the thoughts that I think toward you, says Yahuah, thoughts of peace, and not of evil, to give you an expected end. YIRMEYAHU 29:11-11 את CEPHER

- By whom also we have access by faith into this grace wherein we stand, and rejoice in hope of the glory of Elohiym. And not only so, but we glory in tribulations also: knowing that tribulation works patience; And patience, experience; and experience, hope: And hope makes not ashamed; because the love of Elohiym is shed abroad in our hearts by the Ruach Ha'Qodesh which is given unto us. ROMAIYM 5:2-5 את CEPHER

- Be strong and of a good courage, fear not, nor be afraid of them: for Yahuah Elohayka, he it is that goes with you; he will not fail you, nor forsake you. DEVARIYM 31:6-6 את CEPHER

- But they that wait upon Yahuah shall renew their strength; they shall mount up with wings as eagles; they shall run, and not be weary; and they shall walk, and not faint. YESHA'YAHU 40:31-31 את CEPHER

- Fear not; for I am with you: be not dismayed; for I am your Elohiym: I will strengthen you; yea, I will help you; yea, I will uphold you with the right hand of my righteousness. YESHA'YAHU 41:10-10 את CEPHER

- And now, Adonai, what wait I for? my hope is in you. TEHILLIYM 39:7-7 את CEPHER Yahusha said unto him, If you can believe, all things are possible to him that believes. MARQUS 9:23-23 את CEPHER

- For we are saved by hope: but hope that is seen is not hope: for what a man sees, why does he yet hope for? ROMAIYM 8:24-24 את CEPHER

- For surely there is an end; and your expectation shall not be cut off. MISHLEI 23:18-18 את CEPHER

- But if we hope for that we see not, then do we with patience wait for it. ROMAIYM 8:25-25 את CEPHER NOW faith is the substance of things hoped for, the evidence of things not seen. IVRIYM 11:1-1 את CEPHER

- Blessed is the man that trusts in Yahuah, and whose hope Yahuah is. YIRMEYAHU 17:7-7 את CEPHER

- Finally, brethren, farewell. Be perfect, be of good comfort, be of one mind, live in peace; and the Elohai Ahavah V'Shalom shall be with you. QORINTIYM SHENIY 13:11-11 את CEPHER

- Let him eschew evil, and do good; let him seek peace, and ensue it. KEPHA RI'SHON 3:11-11 את CEPHER
- Be careful for nothing; but in everything by prayer and supplication with thanksgiving let your requests be made known unto Elohiym. And the peace of Elohiym, which passes all understanding, shall keep your hearts and minds through Mashiach Yahusha. PHILIPPIYM 4:6-7 את CEPHER
- I will both lay me down in peace, and sleep: for you, Yahuah, only make me dwell in safety. TEHILLIYM 4:8-8 את CEPHER
- Now Yahuah Shalom himself give you peace always by all means. Yah be with you all. TASLONIQIYM SHENIY (2 THESSALONIANS) 3:16 את CEPHER
- Those things, which ye have both learned, and received, and heard, and seen in me, do: and the Elohai Shalom shall be with you. PHILIPPIYM (PHILIPPIANS) 4:9 את CEPHER
- But the fruit of the Ruach is love, joy, peace, longsuffering, gentleness, goodness, faith, GALATIYM (GALATIANS) 5:22 את CEPHER
- Behold, El is my yeshu`ah; I will trust, and not be afraid: for Yah Yahuah is my strength and my song; he also is become my yeshu`ah. YESHA'YAHU (ISAIAH) 12:2 את CEPHER

TIME TO WALK OUT YOUR HOPE...

- Spiritual affirmations can help you change the way you think about yourself and the world around you.
- You can use affirmations to help you overcome negative self-talk, such as criticism and doubt.
- Make a list of positive affirmations that will help you meet your goals.
- Practice them every day, even if it's just for a few minutes.
- Record yourself saying your affirmations, so you can listen to them later.
- Affirmations are positive affirmations that you can use each day to help boost your confidence and sense of well-being.
- Affirmations can be used as a tool to help you overcome negative feelings, such as anxiety, worry, or anger to banish hope.
- Write a positive affirmation on a piece of paper, post it on the mirror, and say it out loud every day.
- Make a daily habit of looking at the affirmations to brighten your mood and give you hope.

AFFIRMATIONS ABOUT FORGIVENESS

- Rejoicing in hope; patient in tribulation; Forbearing one another, and forgiving one another, if any man have a quarrel against any: even as Mashiach forgave you, so also do ye. QOLASIYM 3:13-13 את CEPHER

- Let the wicked forsake his way, and the unrighteous man his thoughts: and let him return unto El-Yahuah, and he will have mercy upon him; and to our Elohiym, for he will abundantly pardon. YESHA'YAHU 55:7-7 את CEPHER

- And they shall teach no more every man his neighbor, and every man his brother, saying, Know Yahuah: for they shall all know me, from the least of them unto the greatest of them, says Yahuah: for I will forgive their iniquity, and I will remember their sin no more. YIRMEYAHU 31:34-34 את CEPHER

- KNOW ye not, brethren, (for I speak to them that know the Torah,) how that the Torah has dominion over a man as long as he lives? ROMAIYM 7:1-1 את CEPHER

- Then said Yahusha, Father, forgive them; for they know not what they do. And they parted his raiment, and cast lots. LUQAS 23:34-34 את CEPHER

- He that covers his sins shall not prosper: but whoso confesses and forsakes them shall have mercy. MISHLEI 28:13-13 את CEPHER

- I acknowledged my sin unto you, and my iniquity have I not hid. I said, I will confess my transgressions unto Yahuah; and you forgave the iniquity of my sin. Celah. TEHILLIYM 32:5-5 את CEPHER

- Confess your faults one to another, and pray one for another, that ye may be healed. The effectual fervent prayer of a righteous man avails much. YA`AQOV 5:16-16 את CEPHER

- Judge not, and ye shall not be judged: condemn not, and ye shall not be condemned: forgive, and ye shall be forgiven: LUQAS 6:37-37 את CEPHER
- Let all bitterness, and wrath, and anger, and clamor, and evil speaking, be put away from you, with all malice: And be ye kind one to another, tenderhearted, forgiving one another, even as Elohiym for Mashiach's sake has forgiven you. EPH'SIYM 4:31-32 את CEPHER
- For if ye forgive men their transgressions, your heavenly Father will also forgive you: But if ye forgive not men their transgressions, neither will your Father forgive your transgressions. MATTITHYAHU 6:14-15 את CEPHER
- He that covers a transgression seeks love; but he that repeats a matter separates very friends. MISHLEI 17:9-9 את CEPHER
- Then came Kepha to him, and said, Adonai, how oft shall my brother sin against me, and I forgive him? till seven times? Yahusha said unto him, I say not unto you, Until seven times: but, Until seventy times seven. MATTITHYAHU 18:21-22 את CEPHER
- Take heed to yourselves: If your brother trespass against you, rebuke him; and if he repent, forgive him. And if he trespass against you seven times in a day, and seven times in a day turn again to you, saying, I repent; you shall forgive him. LUQAS 17:3-4 את CEPHER

TIME TO WALK OUT YOUR FORGIVENESS...

- Write down a list of things that you have forgiven.
- Make a list of things you can do to forgive someone.
- Make a list of things that make it difficult to forgive someone.
- Make a list of all the things you are grateful for.
- Write down 3 positive daily spiritual affirmations about forgiveness.
- Write down 3 things you need to forgive yourself for.
- If you have a spiritual belief system or a belief in the Most High, it's important to learn how to forgive the people who have wronged you.
- Forgiveness is a spiritual principle.
- Forgiveness can help to relieve guilt.
- Forgiveness can help to relieve stress and anxiety.
- Forgiveness can help you to let go of negative emotions.
- Forgiveness can help you to move on.
- These affirmations can be a great way to help people who are struggling with addiction, self-harm, and other negative behaviors.
- These affirmations can be used as a tool to cope with grief or the loss of a loved one.
- Parents can use these daily affirmations with their children to help them build a positive relationship and explore the power of forgiveness in their own lives.

AFFIRMATIONS ABOUT PEACE

- Finally, brethren, farewell. Be perfect, be of good comfort, be of one mind, live in peace; and the Elohai Ahavah V'Shalom shall be with you. QORINTIYM SHENIY 13:11-11 את CEPHER
- Let him eschew evil, and do good; let him seek peace, and ensue it. KEPHA RI'SHON 3:11-11 את CEPHER
- Be careful for nothing; but in everything by prayer and supplication with thanksgiving let your requests be made known unto Elohiym. And the peace of Elohiym, which passes all understanding, shall keep your hearts and minds through Mashiach Yahusha. PHILIPPIYM 4:6-7 את CEPHER
- I will both lay me down in peace, and sleep: for you, Yahuah, only make me dwell in safety. TEHILLIYM 4:8-8 את CEPHER
- Now Yahuah Shalom himself give you peace always by all means. Yah be with you all. TASLONIQIYM SHENIY (2 THESSALONIANS) 3:16 את CEPHER
- Those things, which ye have both learned, and received, and heard, and seen in me, do: and the Elohai Shalom shall be with you. PHILIPPIYM (PHILIPPIANS) 4:9 את CEPHER
- But the fruit of the Ruach is love, joy, peace, longsuffering, gentleness, goodness, faith, GALATIYM (GALATIANS) 5:22 את CEPHER
- Behold, El is my yeshu`ah; I will trust, and not be afraid: for Yah Yahuah is my strength and my song; he also is become my yeshu`ah. YESHA'YAHU (ISAIAH) 12:2 את CEPHER
- And let the peace of Elohiym rule in your hearts, to the which also ye are called in one body; and be ye thankful. QOLASIYM (COLOSSIANS) 3:15 את CEPHER
- THEREFORE being justified by faith, we have peace with Elohiym through our Adonai Yahusha Ha'Mashiach: ROMAIYM (ROMANS) 5:1 את CEPHER
- For to be carnally minded is death; but to be spiritually

minded is life and peace. ROMAIYM (ROMANS) 8:6 את CEPHER

- Blessed are the peacemakers: for they shall be called the children of Elohiym. MATTITHYAHU (MATTHEW) 5:9 את CEPHER
- And, ye adoniym, do the same things unto them, forbearing threatening: knowing that your Adonai also is in heaven; neither is there respect of persons with him. EPH'SIYM (EPHESIANS) 6:9 את CEPHER
- You will guard him in perfect peace, whose mind is stayed on you: because he trusts in you. YESHA'YAHU (ISAIAH) 26:3 את CEPHER

TIME TO WALK OUT YOUR PEACE...

- One of the best things you can do for yourself is to get in touch with your spiritual side. One of the best ways to do this is to practice daily spiritual affirmations about peace in your life.
- There are many different ways to do this, but the most effective way is through meditation and visualization.
- You can start by selecting a quiet place to sit comfortably with your eyes closed.
- You can then begin by breathing deeply and slowly, focusing on your breathing and clearing your mind of any other thoughts.
- You can then focus on what you want by saying your affirmation out loud, in the present tense.
- If you want more peace in your life, you might say something like "I am at peace with everyone around me".
- Practice yoga or meditation for 10-20 minutes every day to connect with your inner self and find peace within.
- Start your day with a gratitude journal and write down everything you are thankful for.
- Smile at strangers when you walk by them and make eye contact - this will boost your mood and theirs as well.
- Volunteer at a local charity - this will help you connect with those around you and feel better about yourself.
- Use positive affirmations in the morning and throughout the day to remind yourself of the positive things in your life.
- Spend time with loved ones or friends that make you feel good - this will help to remind you that you are always supported no matter what.

AFFIRMATIONS ABOUT CONFIDENCE/SELF-ESTEEM

- Have not I commanded you? Be strong and of a good courage; be not afraid, neither be dismayed: for Yahuah Elohayka is with you whithersoever you go. YAHUSHA (JOSHUA) 1:9 את CEPHER

- Blessed is the man that trusts in Yahuah, and whose hope Yahuah is. YIRMEYAHU (JEREMIAH) 17:7 את CEPHER

- Though a host should encamp against me, my heart shall not fear: though war should rise against me, in this will I be confident. TEHILLIYM (PSALMS) 27:3 את CEPHER

- For you have possessed my mind: you have covered me in my mother's womb. I will praise you; for I am fearfully and wonderfully made: marvellous are your works; and that my soul knows right well. TEHILLIYM (PSALMS) 139:13-14 את CEPHER

- With him is an arm of flesh; but with us is Yahuah Elohaynu to help us, and to fight our battles. And the people rested themselves upon the words of Yechizqiyahu king of Yahudah. DIVREI HAYAMIYM SHENIY (2 CHRONICLES) 32:8 את CEPHER

- And the work of righteousness shall be peace; and the effect of righteousness quietness and assurance forever. YESHA'YAHU (ISAIAH) 32:17 את CEPHER

- But they that wait upon Yahuah shall renew their strength; they shall mount up with wings as eagles; they shall run, and not be weary; and they shall walk, and not faint. YESHA'YAHU (ISAIAH) 40:31 את CEPHER

- Fear not; for I am with you: be not dismayed; for I am your Elohiym: I will strengthen you; yea, I will help you; yea, I will uphold you with the right hand of my righteousness. YESHA'YAHU (ISAIAH) 41:10 את CEPHER

- Being confident of this very thing, that he which has begun a good work in you will perform it until the day of Yahusha Ha'Mashiach: PHILIPPIYM (PHILIPPIANS) 1:6 את CEPHER

- I can do all things through Mashiach which strengthens me. PHILIPPIYM (PHILIPPIANS) 4:13 את CEPHER

- In whom we have boldness and access with confidence by faith in him. EPH'SIYM (EPHESIANS) 3:12 את CEPHER

- And I was with you in weakness, and in fear, and in much trembling. And my speech and my preaching was not with enticing words of man's wisdom, but in demonstration of the Ruach and of power: That your faith should not stand in the wisdom of men, but in the power of Elohiym. QORINTIYM RI'SHON (1 CORINTHIANS) 2:3-5 את CEPHER

- To another faith by the same Ruach; to another the gifts of healing by the same Ruach; QORINTIYM RI'SHON (1 CORINTHIANS) 12:9 את CEPHER

- Let us therefore come boldly unto the throne of grace, that we may obtain mercy, and find grace to help in time of need. IVRIYM (HEBREWS) 4:16 את CEPHER

TIME TO WALK OUT YOUR CONFIDENCE/ SELF-ESTEEM...

- Confidence is a choice. It's up to you to choose to be confident.
- Your level of confidence is based on the choices you make and how you treat yourself.
- You're your own worst enemy. Don't let yourself get in your own way by thinking negative thoughts.
- Practice makes perfect. The more you work at something, the better you'll get at it.
- Don't compare yourself to others. Everyone is different so you shouldn't expect to be the same as everyone else.
- You can't please everyone, so don't even try.
- Stay grateful for all that you have.
- Accept who you are and be in your own skin.
- Be confident in your own skin.
- Love yourself and treat yourself well.
- Be grateful for the little things in life that make you smile.
- Make time for yourself every day.

AFFIRMATIONS ABOUT JOY

- Rejoice evermore. Pray without ceasing. In everything give thanks: for this is the will of Elohiym in Mashiach Yahusha concerning you. TASLONIQIYM RI'SHON (1 THESSALONIANS) 5:16-18 את CEPHER
- Yahuah Elohayka in the midst of you is mighty; he will save, he will rejoice over you with joy; he will rest in his love, he will joy over you with singing. TSEPHANYAHU (ZEPHANIAH) 3:17 את CEPHER
- Rejoicing in hope; patient in tribulation; continuing instant in prayer; ROMAIYM (ROMANS) 12:12 את CEPHER
- My brethren, count it all joy when ye fall into diverse temptations; Knowing this, that the trying of your faith works patience. YA`AQOV 1:2-3 את CEPHER
- O clap your hands, all ye people; shout unto Elohiym with the voice of triumph. TEHILLIYM 47:1-1 את CEPHER
- You have multiplied the nation, and not increased the joy: they joy before you according to the joy in harvest, and as men rejoice when they divide the spoil. YESHA'YAHU 9:3-3 את CEPHER
- Go your way, eat your bread with joy, and drink your wine with a merry heart; for Elohiym now accepts your works. QOHELETH 9:7-7 את CEPHER
- The hope of the righteous shall be gladness: but the expectation of the wicked shall perish. MISHLEI 10:28-28 את CEPHER
- Whom having not seen, ye love; in whom, though now ye see him not, yet believing, ye rejoice with joy unspeakable and full of glory: Receiving the end of your faith, even the salvation of your souls. KEPHA RI'SHON 1:8-9 את CEPHER
- Now the Elohiym of hope fill you with all joy and peace in believing, that ye may abound in hope, through the power of

the Ruach Ha'Qodesh. ROMAIYM 15:13-13 את CEPHER

- Having many things to write unto you, I would not write with paper and ink: but I trust to come unto you, and speak face to face, that our joy may be full. YOCHANON SHENIY 1:12-12 את CEPHER

- I say unto you, that likewise joy shall be in heaven over one sinner that repents, more than over ninety and nine just persons, which need no repentance. LUQAS 15:7-7 את CEPHER

- Then he said unto them, Go your way, eat the fat, and drink the sweet, and send portions unto them for whom nothing is prepared: for this day is holy unto our Adonai: neither be ye sorry; for the joy of Yahuah is your strength. EZRA V'NECHEMYAHU 8:10-10 את CEPHER

- And in every province, and in every city, whithersoever the king's commandment and his decree came, the Yahudiym had joy and gladness, a feast and a good day. And many of the people of the land became Yahudiym; for the fear of the Yahudiym fell upon them. ECTER 8:17-17 את CEPHER

TIME TO WALK OUT YOUR JOY...

- Happiness is a choice.
- You have the power to turn negative thoughts into positive ones.
- Joy is an emotion that comes from within.
- It's important to spend time alone to reflect and connect with your inner self.
- Accept your flaws and practice being kind to yourself.
- Spend time with others that you trust, who are also positive influences on your life.
- Create a regular routine of exercise to get some physical activity in every day.
- Practice gratitude every day to remind yourself of all that you have to be thankful for.
- Write down a list of your current joys.
- Write down the things that make you feel grateful.
- Write down one thing you can do today to appreciate your life more.

ACKNOWLEDGEMENT

I would like to take this time to acknowledge my Heavenly Father, and the Founder of my faith, The Most High, Y_h, of which there would be no affirmation or word. I want to also thank my husband, Apostle Jimmie Williams, for his patience, wisdom and understanding. You are my rock and best friend. Thank you! I want to thank my dear sister, Yahvette Richardson for her input and wisdom. You are a Proverbs 31 woman and a Y_h send! I love you my friend and sister. I want to acknowledge my family, specifically my brother, Ray Chambers. You are an angel and the reason this book was written. This is a positive book of affirmations that was inspired by the amount of people you touch in a positive way.

9 798351 718996